THIS BOOK
BELONGS TO:

Apple

Apples are the fruit of apple trees and part of the rose family. Apples are one of the most widely grown tree fruits. Apples have an outer peel that is smooth and shiny and comes in shades of red, yellow and green. Though apples come in a variety of colors their inner flesh is always white. Each apple has five distinct seed pockets called carpels, but the number of seeds depends on the variety and health of the tree.

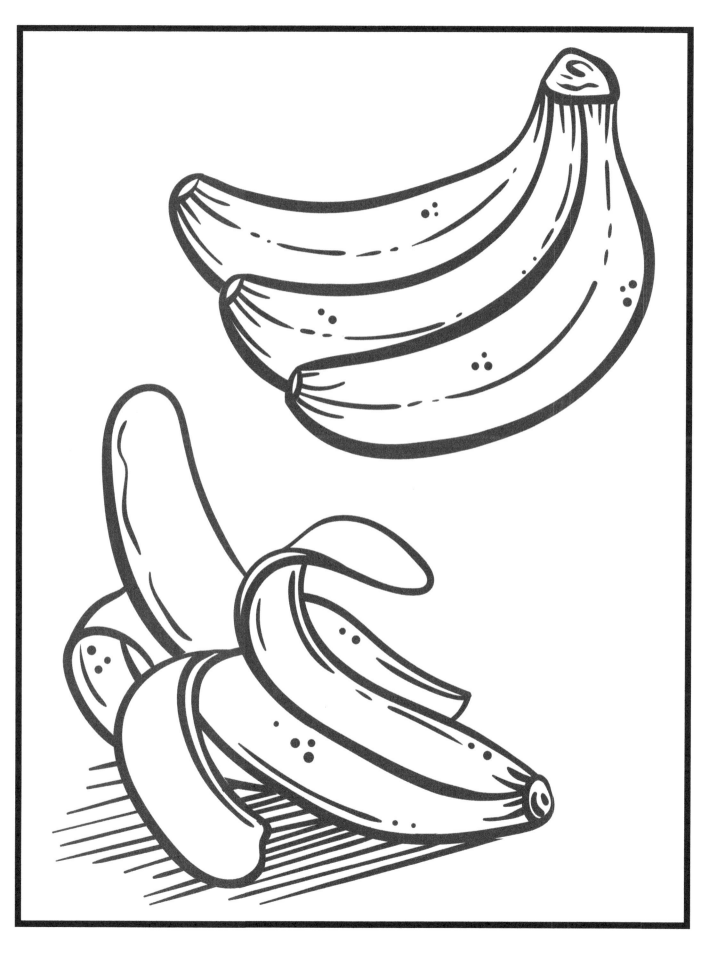

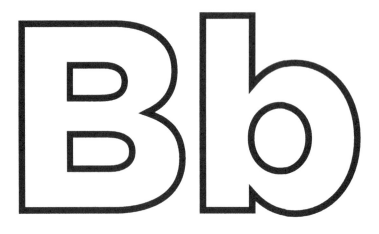

Banana

Bananas are the fruit produced by banana plants and grow in large, hanging bunches. Banana plants are not trees but a type of herb. A row of bananas is sometimes called a "hand," a single banana is called a "finger." As the bananas grow and ripen, their outer peel turns from green to yellow.

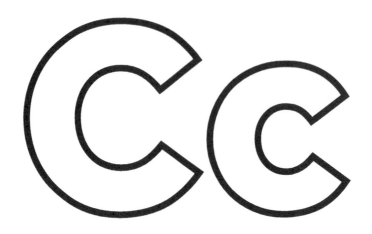

Carrot

The carrot is a root vegetable. This means they grow underground and absorb a great amount of nutrients from the soil. The carrot is usually orange in color although purple, red, white, and yellow varieties also exist. It is always a good idea to cut the greens off when you harvest carrots because the tops will continue to grow, leaching water and nutrients out of the carrots.

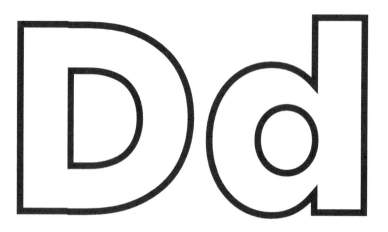

Date

Dates are small, sweet fruits that grow in large bunches on a date palm tree. A single bunch may contain as many as 1,000 dates. Date palms can be found in hot, dry climates. When dates are ripe, their color changes from yellow green to golden brown to black. Dates contain one long, slender seed, called a stone.

Eggplant

Eggplants belong to the nightshade family. Their fruit is known for their elongated egg shape and vibrant shiny purple skin, but some eggplants are perfectly egg shaped and can come in white, green, lavender and rose. Just like tomatoes, in botany an eggplant is classified as a berry, but in cooking an eggplant is considered to be a vegetable for its savory taste and culinary uses.

Fig

Figs grow on a fig tree and are called fruits, but they are actually inside-out flowers. They are small and pear-shaped with a sweet, nutty flavor and chewy texture. Today people eat figs fresh or dried, but most figs sold in stores are dried because the fruit spoils very easily. People have been growing figs since at least 5000 BC. They were an important source of food for the ancient Greeks and Romans.

Grapefruit

The Grapefruit is a tart, juicy citrus fruit that grows in trees. The grapefruit, like other citrus fruits, has a juicy pulp inside a leathery skin. Oranges are also citrus fruits, but the grapefruit is larger and has a more sour taste. The grapefruit outer rind is a yellow orange and the soft pulp inside can be light yellow, pink, or red.

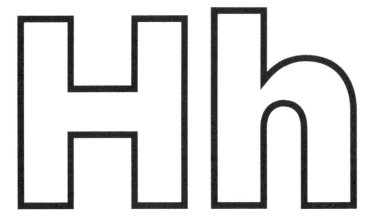

Honey

Honey is a food made by honey bees from nectar, a liquid made by flowers and plants. One bee will visit between 50-500 flowers per day, then place the honey into honeycombs for storage and fermentation. A beehive produces 90 pounds of honey, but takes 40,000 bees to produce it. Honey is the only food which is made by insects, but eaten by both insects and humans.

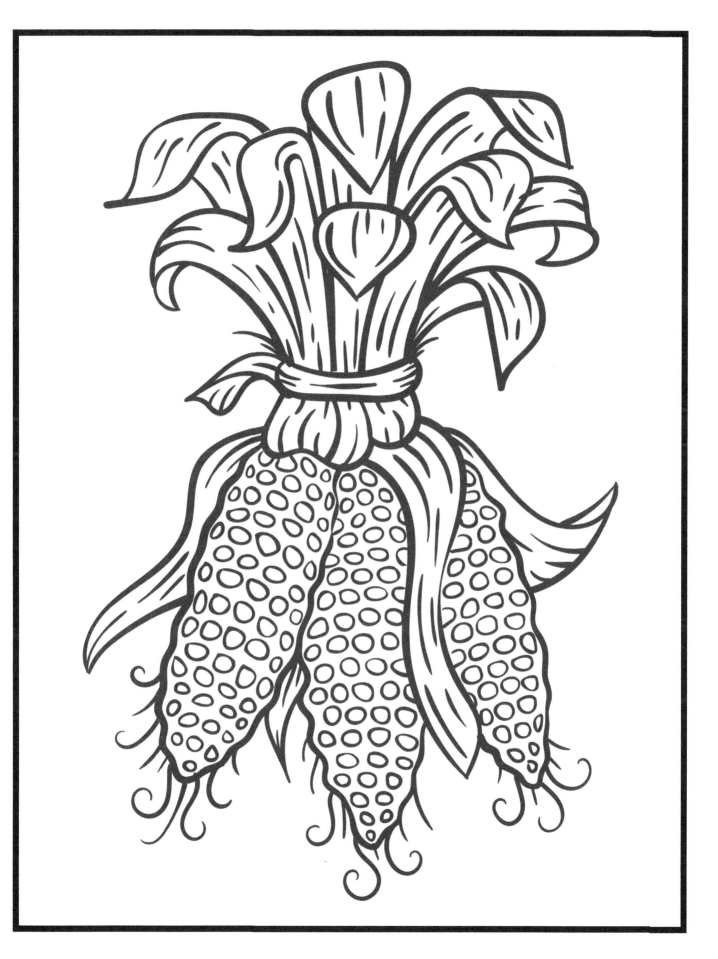

Indian corn

Indian corn or flint corn is a variant of maize. Maize (corn) is a cereal crop that is part of the grass family. In the US, corn is characterized as a vegetable, but in many parts of the world corn is considered a grain. Indian corn is known for its hard outer shell kernels, which come in a multitude of colors. You often see Indian corn used in fall decorations because of the multicolored kernels representing all the harvest and fall colors.

Jalapeño

The jalapeño is a type of Mexican pepper. It is in the chili family and prized for the hot, burning sensation that it produces in the mouth when eaten. The jalapeño is commonly picked and consumed while still green, but it is occasionally allowed to fully ripen and turn red, orange, or yellow.

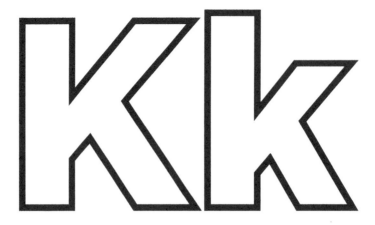

Kiwi

The kiwi fruit is a berry that grows on several species of woody vines. The kiwis are dioecious, meaning male and female flowers are born on separate plants and only the female vines produce the kiwi fruits. The kiwi is oval-shaped with furry brown outer skin that is edible, but it is usually removed. The inside is a vibrant green with small black seeds circling a lighter colored center.

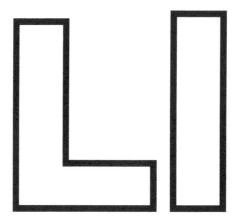

Lemon & Lime

Lemons and limes are a citrus fruits that grow on trees. Lemons have yellow leathery outer skin color and limes have a leathery green color. The lemon and lime trees are evergreen trees. They bloom and produce fruit all year round. They both have a sour taste, because the juice contains about 5-6% citric acid.

Mushroom

Mushrooms are a fungus. Unlike plants, mushrooms do not require sunlight to make energy. The mushroom is a very nutritious food and is used in many cuisines. They are often referred to as the "meat" of the vegetable world. Most mushrooms for human consumption are grown in a controlled, sterilized environment. There are a few mushroom varieties found in the wild that are highly poisonous, so do not risk collecting and eating mushrooms in the wild.

Nn

Nectarine

Nectarines belong to the same species as peaches and are stone fruits that grow on deciduous trees. Though the nectarine is the same species as peaches, they are regarded commercially as different fruits. Nectarines have a smooth yellow and red skin, whereas peaches have a fuzzy yellow and orange skin.

Olive

Olives are the fruit of the olive tree and an important food crop in countries around the Mediterranean Sea. Olive oil is the juice made by crushing olives to be used as a cooking oil. The degree of ripeness determines the color of olives at harvest. Green olives are picked when they are full size, but before the ripening cycle has begun, they are usually a shade of green to yellow. Black olives are picked at full maturity and fully ripe. They are found in assorted shades of purple to brown to black.

Pear

Pears are similar to apples in that they are part of the rose family and have small seeds and grow on trees. They often have a teardrop shape and can have a green, red, yellow, or brown skin. They are often picked before they are ripe and ripen best off the tree at room temperature. Pears used to be called "butter fruit" for their soft, butter-like texture.

Quinoa

Quinoa is considered a whole grain, although it is technically a seed. Quinoa is a protein-rich seed from a vegetable that belongs to the family of Swiss chard, spinach and beets. Quinoa might just be one of the healthiest foods on the planet as it has eight amino acids and many other nutrients. It is so nutritious that NASA has recommended it for for food on space flights and the United Nations has suggested it be used for feeding people in areas where food is scarce.

Raspberry

A raspberry is an aggregate fruit, meaning it has many parts joined together. Raspberries are usually red, purple, or black. They grow on prickly bushes called brambles. These bushes produce small flowers that develop into the berries and are attached to a firm core. When a raspberry is picked, the core stays on the plant and this is why a picked raspberry is hollow on the inside. Raspberries are similar to blackberries. but when a blackberry is picked, the core stays inside the fruit.

Strawberry

A strawberry is a plant that grows fruit. The fruit of the strawberry is the thickened part of the stem called receptacles with edible seeds on the outside. Strawberries when ripe are bright red, juicy and very sweet, but unlike some other fruits, they do not continue to ripen after being picked.

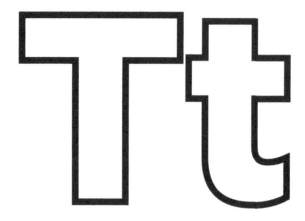

Tomato

Tomatoes are the fruit of the tomato plant. Because the tomato has seeds and grows from a flowering plant, botanically they are a fruit, not a vegetable. In 1887, the status of tomatoes became a matter of legal importance, as the US tariff laws imposed a duty on vegetables, but not fruits. The US Supreme Court ruled that tomatoes were to be considered vegetables based on the popular definition that classified vegetables by savory flavor and use.

Ugli
(Tangelo)

Ugli fruit, also known as the tangelo, is a citrus fruit hybrid. This fruit is a hybrid of a grapefruit, orange, and tangerine. It is a large sweet juicy fruit with greenish-yellow thick wrinkled skin. It started to grow quickly all across Jamaica and is named ugli fruit because of it ugly appearance.

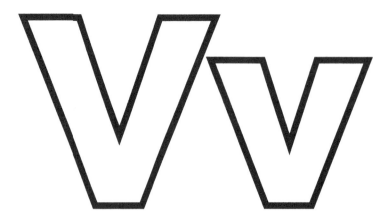

Vanilla

Vanilla is a spice and flavoring that is one of the most popular ingredients in food. Vanilla grows on an orchid vine and is one of the few orchids that actually produce fruit. Vanilla is made from the seeds inside the vanilla bean pods. While the beans are being harvested, they are soaked in hot water, then laid out in the sun to dry before cutting the pods and scraping out the seeds.

Ww

Watermelon

Watermelon is a large, sweet fruit that grows on spreading vines along the ground. The watermelon is part of the gourd family and is almost entirely water. They are the second largest fruit in the world, second only to the Jackfruit. They have a striped green thick outer rind with a bright red interior and black seeds. Though they were originally native to West Africa, they are now grown world wide.

Ximenia

Ximenia Is a small sprawling tree in the tropics that produces fruit. The fruits are small, only about 1.25 inches (3cm) long, and will ripen to lemon-yellow or orange red with one seed in every fruit. Ximenia fruits have a unique flavor, and depending on the fruit, the flavor can range from a bitter almond-like flavor to very sweet. It has a sticky texture, but the flowers can have an intense lilac smell. Birds love this fruit.

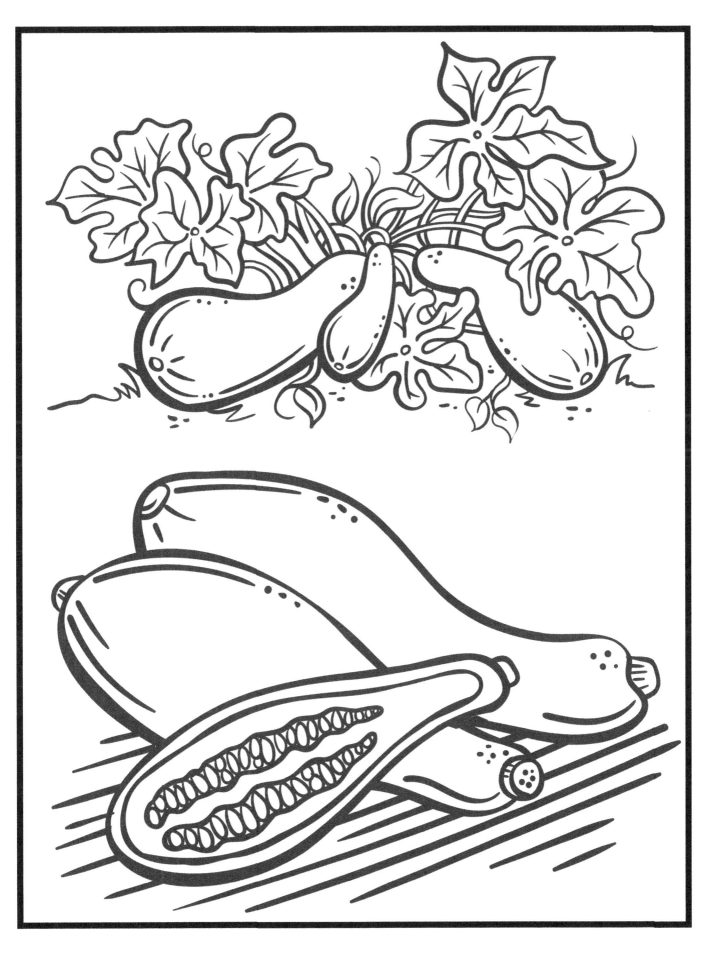

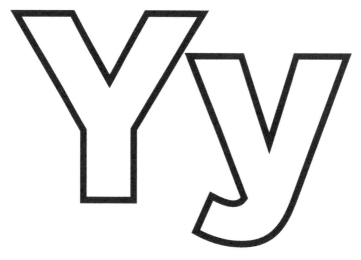

Yellow Squash

Yellow squash is a type of summer squash that belongs to the pumpkin family. Summer squash, like zucchini, have thin skins and can be eaten whole - skin, seeds, and all. Winter squashs like pumpkin and butternut squash have robust harder skins that are not usually edible and their seeds generally need to be removed before eating. The yellow squash comes in two varieties, straight neck and crook neck. Both varieties have fatter bottoms and taper toward the neck.

Zz

Zucchini

Zucchini is a type of summer squash that belongs to the pumpkin family. The fruit of the zucchini has a green outer skin with a creamy white inside filled with numerous tiny edible seeds. The zucchini blooms early in the summer with yellow-colored flowers that attract bees which it requires for pollination. The zucchini blossoms are edible and are often fried or stuffed.

Made in the USA
Middletown, DE
05 November 2022